Monarchs

Monarchs

KATHRYN LASKY

photographs by
Christopher G. Knight

A Gulliver Green Book

Harcourt Brace & Company

SAN DIEGO   NEW YORK   LONDON

The photographs that appear
on pages 20–21, 22–23, 44, and 46–47
were taken by William H. Calvert.
Used by permission.

Library of Congress Cataloging-in-Publication Data
Monarchs/text by Kathryn Lasky;
photographs by Christopher G. Knight. — 1st ed.
p.   cm.
"Gulliver books."
Summary: Describes the life cycle and winter migrations
of the eastern and western monarch butterflies and the two towns
that protect their winter habitats.
ISBN 0-15-255296-0. — ISBN 0-15-255297-9 (pbk.)
1. Monarch butterfly — Migration — Juvenile literature.
2. Monarch butterfly — Wintering — Juvenile literature.
[1. Monarch butterfly. 2. Butterflies.]
I. Knight, Christopher G., ill. II. Title.
QL561.D3L36   1993
595.78'9 — dc20   92-33972

First edition

A B C D E   A B C D E (pbk.)

Printed in Singapore

The display type was set in Bernhard Modern by Thompson Type, San Diego, California.
The text type was set in Meridien by Thompson Type, San Diego, California.
Color separations by Bright Arts, Ltd., Singapore
Printed and bound by Tien Wah Press, Singapore
Production supervision by Warren Wallerstein and Kent MacElwee
Designed by Linda Lockowitz

We would like to thank the following for their
participation and invaluable help in making this book:
Ro Vaccaro, president of the Friends of the Monarch; Ms. Klevan
and her entire kindergarten class in Pacific Grove; Chris, Annette,
and Karl Lindstrom; Dr. Lincoln Brower; Dr. William Calvert;
the people of El Rosario in the state of Michoacán, Mexico;
and the citizens of Pacific Grove, California, who voted
to save the threatened grove by purchasing it and
thus preventing further development.

The Cubbyhole

IN A BAY off the coast of Maine there is an island with a cove on its northeast side. At the head of this cove is a deep notch between the rocks, like a cubbyhole, that is wind-safe and cozy. On one side of the notch a pine forest grows right down to the water's edge; on the other side the rocks give way to marsh grass growing thick and pale. Here the land dips to a swale sprigged with wildflowers and a tangle of sea roses, called rugosas. It then climbs steeply upward to a dirt road where a thick stand of milkweed grows. A monarch butterfly has lighted on the leaf of a milkweed and has squeezed out a single egg, white and shiny, no bigger than the head of a pin. She flies off to another leaf, where she lays another egg. A single female can lay approximately four hundred eggs.

The little egg is very tough. A summer gale with pelting rain and scouring winds blows from the northeast and invades the usually wind-safe cove. Trees are ripped up and the marsh grass tosses wildly about, but the little egg stays on the leaf of the wind-bent milkweed plants.

Within a few days the egg hatches. The larva is so tiny — about one twenty-fifth of an inch long — it is barely visible to the naked eye. At one end of its grayish white body is a black dot perhaps one hundredth of an inch across. Amazingly, this is the head. And on this little head is a mouth one thousandth of an inch wide, and near this mouth is a pair of very short antennae that help the larva sense its way around a milkweed leaf. A pair of long black filaments near the front of the caterpillar and a shorter pair near the rear of its body are not antennae. They are used like small whips or clubs when the caterpillar twists its body about in defense against predators.

The tiny caterpillar also has eight pairs of legs. The front three pairs have small claws that help grab leaves for eating. The back five pairs, called prolegs, are stubbier and have hooks, or crotchets, which help the caterpillar cling and move along stems and leaves. When the caterpillar becomes a butterfly, the first three pairs of legs will become the butterfly's legs, while the prolegs will shrivel and disappear.

The larva's first meal is often its own egg case. Its next meal might be the hairlike filaments covering the surface of the milkweed leaf. Then it will begin on the leaf itself. All day and all night it munches, pausing only occasionally to rest. Milkweed is the only food that monarch caterpillars eat. For many other animals, especially birds, milkweed is poisonous. If they do not die from eating it, they get very sick. The poisons that accumulate in the bodies of the caterpillars, and later the butterflies, provide a natural defense against such predators as blue jays and other birds that might otherwise try to eat them.

After three days of almost nonstop eating, the little caterpillar has grown too big for its own skin. It stops and fastens itself to a leaf with a bit of silk produced from the spinneret just below its mouth. A shiver ripples through the caterpillar as it begins its first molt, or shedding of old skin. At this stage the old skin is as hard as a fingernail, and it splits down the middle of the caterpillar's back. The caterpillar will molt four or five times over the next few weeks, and with each molt it will grow bigger, adding more yellow and black stripes to its body.

After two weeks of eating, the caterpillar is now two inches long and is more than 2,700 times its original weight. If a six-pound human baby grew as fast as a caterpillar, it would weigh eight tons in twelve days. The caterpillar finally stops eating. For its next development stage it can travel

to any twig or branch or stay on a milkweed plant. But wherever it goes, the caterpillar will climb straight up. Once it has decided on a spot, it produces more silk and weaves a button on the twig or branch it has chosen. Near the rear legs of the caterpillar is a tiny hook-shaped structure called a cremaster. The caterpillar stabs the cremaster into the silk button and wriggles hard to see if it will hold. If it does, the caterpillar seems to relax and hangs from the silk button. Within minutes, the head curls up and the caterpillar looks like the letter J. For several hours it will stay this way, preparing for its final molt. Then the skin begins to split as the caterpillar twists and shivers, and as this last skin splits off, the bright bands of yellow and black dissolve into a milky green sheath called a chrysalis. Because the chrysalis seems to wrap itself around the form of the butterfly in the same way an infant is wrapped in swaddling clothes, this period of development is often called the pupal stage, from the Latin word *pupa* meaning "doll."

Within a short time the chrysalis hardens into a beautiful jade-green case studded with gold dots. It hangs like an exquisite magic lantern, inside which marvelous, seemingly magical changes are occurring. The body of the caterpillar melts away into a solution of transforming cells and tissues. Inside the chrysalis, the metamorphosis from caterpillar to butterfly takes approximately fifteen days.

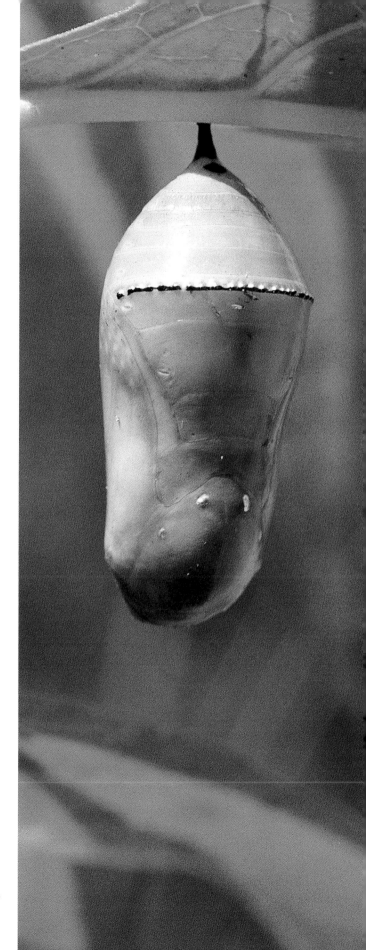

New Wings Shimmer in the Sunlight

CLARA WATERMAN is in a hurry to leave her store on North Haven Island in Penobscot Bay, Maine. But this morning the mail boat from the mainland has come and is turning right around for the return trip. All the supplies for the Waterman store have to be unloaded double-quick. At eighty-two Clara can beg off unloading thirty-pound crates of Georgia peaches and cases of soft drinks, but it means she has to stay on the cash register while the others unload the boat. Then everybody in town starts craving the big fat peaches as soon as they see them on the dock. Soon the line of customers at the Waterman store practically goes out the door.

Clara isn't going to be able to go home at noon as planned. She knew she should have brought the chrysalis down to the store in the morning and set it right by the cash register. Now she'll probably miss it hatching out. She has seen hundreds of monarchs hatch out in her lifetime, and she never tires of it. For Clara there is only one thing better than seeing a butterfly emerge, and that is watching a child see it hatch. It's almost as if two miracles are happening at the same time — the emerging butterfly and the wonder in the child's face.

The morning following the arrival of the peaches at the Waterman store, five children from another island come over to North Haven to talk to Clara about butterflies. She wants to take them to the cubbyhole where the milkweed grows so they can look for caterpillars. Maybe there will even be some chrysalises they can take home to watch hatch.

Monarch chrysalises hatch just about anyplace. All summer long Clara brings home bunches of milkweed that are crawling with caterpillars. She props the branches in jars filled with water to keep the plants fresh and builds little shoebox terrariums to put the jars in. When the chrysalises hatch, Clara releases the butterflies into her yard. Sometimes she

just puts the jars of milkweed on a table or a bookshelf. And caterpillars can travel! She remembers a summer years ago when she was a young girl. She went up to her closet to get out her best dress for a party and found a chrysalis hanging from the sash.

When the children come to Clara's house, they are amazed to see where the caterpillars have crept to form their chrysalises.

"That one just flew off before sunset last night," Clara says, pointing straight up at the door frame as they walk into her kitchen. An empty chrysalis, dry and transparent, quivers in the noon breeze. The children spot another chrysalis that has not yet hatched on the handle of a pail in the sink.

And out on the porch a small darkened lantern hangs from the leaf of a potted milkweed plant. Inside this chrysalis is an orange glimmer like the flame of a flickering candle: the wings of the monarch. The chrysalis shakes

and begins to split. Within minutes a new monarch has hatched. Wet and crumpled, it seems completely exhausted. But soon the monarch begins pumping fluid from its swollen body into its wings.

"Maybe it will fly away while we're here." Clara's voice swells with excitement. The children press around her. She explains that before the butterfly flies off, its feeding tube, or proboscis, must be assembled. The proboscis is a hollow tube through which the butterfly sucks nectar and water. When the butterfly first hatches, the two parts forming the proboscis are not yet interlocked, and until they are, the butterfly cannot feed. When the butterfly is not drinking nectar, the proboscis coils up under its head like a watch spring.

Gradually, over an hour's time, the once wrinkled and wet wings begin to spread, becoming bright and velvety. The children look closely. The edges of the wings are bordered in black with a double row of white spots. The body of the butterfly also has white spots. A web of black veins spreads across the orange wings, making them as bright as stained-glass windows with the sun shining through. This monarch is a female. If it were a male, it would have a single black dot on each hind wing.

The colors and patterns of a butterfly's wings are made by tens of thousands of microscopically small flat scales that overlap like shingles on a roof. If the scales are rubbed off, which can happen, the wing underneath is bare and colorless. The butterfly can still fly, however, even missing a few scales.

On either side of the butterfly's head is a compound eye, which is actually many little eyes pressed into one. These little individual eyes have six sides and are called facets. The two compound eyes of the monarch are made up of thousands of these facets. So instead of seeing one image, a butterfly sees thousands of little images. Compound eyes are very good at detecting movement as well as perceiving a wide range of colors, which helps the butterfly find nectar-rich flowers.

"It's getting ready!" Clara's voice trembles with anticipation. The butterfly's wings shimmer in the noon sun, there is a quiver, and then silently it lifts into gentle fluttering flight.

On Spirals of Wind

A T NIGHT, long after she has taken the children to the cubbyhole to collect caterpillars and chrysalises, Clara Waterman thinks about the magic that is still happening under her own roof. Three more chrysalises have begun to darken, and she can see perfectly developed butterflies inside them. This stage is called the imago, because the image of the adult butterfly that will hatch in the next several hours can be seen in the transparent shell.

The monarchs that hatch at the end of summer are called migrant butterflies. Different from the earlier summer and spring monarchs that live only four or five weeks, the migrants will live for several months. Also unlike the earlier monarchs, the migrants are not sexually mature and will not immediately mate and reproduce. Instead they will wait until spring, saving their energy and fat supply for the long and mysterious journey south for the winter.

The butterfly that flew off when the children were visiting Clara's garden will soon begin its migration south. It will join other monarchs coming from as far north as Canada and as far west as the Great Lakes and even the Rocky Mountains. Their final destination is a place they have never been to, a place that only their great-great-grandparents have visited. It is over two thousand miles away in Mexico.

All the late summer monarchs east of the Rocky Mountains migrate to Mexico. Nobody knows how they do it. Scientists have been studying monarchs' flight, trying to figure out how they find their way to the mountain ranges in Mexico where they spend the winter. No previous ancestor of a monarch has lived long enough to tell them. Is there perhaps a scent left? A trail marked? Do they have little computers in their

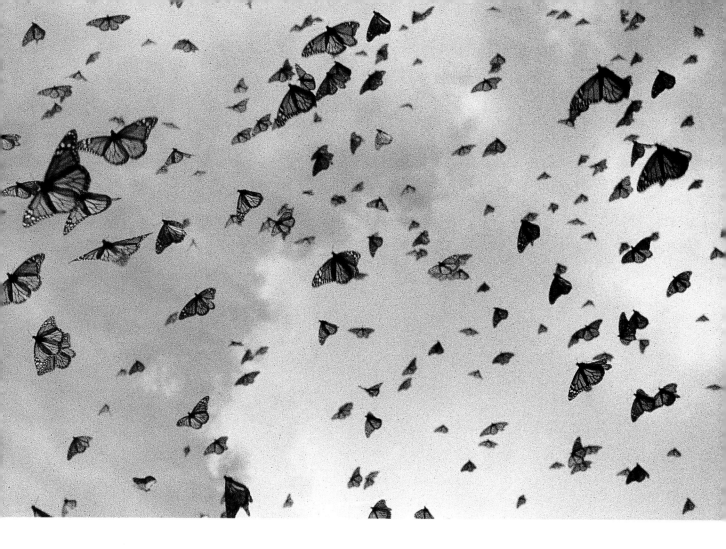

heads that help them navigate? How can a tiny insect that weighs less than a gram fly all the way to Mexico from Canada? It is one of the great mysteries of science. The monarchs west of the Rockies migrate to several sites in California to spend the winter. This migration is not nearly as large nor as long as the flight to Mexico, but it is equally mystifying.

What is known is that all monarchs are expert gliders. On spirals of wind sweeping down from Canada the skillful eastern fliers catch rides to their wintering grounds in Mexico. They will even wait in trees at the edge of the sea for a favorable wind to carry them across large gulfs and bays. They come in waves, or pulses, of thousands and tens of thousands. One minute the sky will be blank; the next minute legions of monarchs appear like sparkling rivers in the sky. Flying at speeds up to twenty miles per hour, they catch thermal updrafts, vigorous columns of warm air that give them free rides. And if there is a crosswind, the butterfly often turns its body sideways, partly into the breeze, to compensate for downwind drift. Pilots of airplanes do this all the time. Monarchs have been doing it longer.

Nobody knows for certain just how long monarchs have been migrating. Some believe it started during the last ice age ten thousand years ago when the monarchs began to migrate in search of milkweed. Only on milkweed will the females lay their eggs. The monarch's scientific name, *Danaus plexippus*, means "milkweed butterfly." It is thought that thousands of years ago milkweed plants grew only in the regions of Mexico and farther south. Then gradually this plant started to creep northward, possibly following the retreat of glaciers and cold weather. The monarchs followed this northerly movement of the plant, and their migrations

began. Now, during the warmer months, the first, second, and third generations of monarchs fly north, following the fields of milkweed. But because the monarch is by origin a tropical creature, it cannot withstand the severe winters of the north. Therefore, every autumn the butterflies born in August, the fourth-generation migrants, fly south to a warmer climate for a kind of hibernation, or light winter sleep. Because of their inactivity they can conserve energy and survive to mate in the spring, when the new fields of milkweed bloom, producing a new generation of butterflies.

The compass course for Mexico for the monarchs east of the Rocky Mountains is 210–220 southwest. It is a flight that takes them over forests and meadows, dusty desert towns and steel skyscrapers, volcanoes and mountain ranges.

Before the afternoon light fades, the migrating butterflies begin to search for the colors of nectar flowers — the blue of a foxglove, the yellow of a buttercup, or the bright orange of a marigold. Monarchs are especially drawn to purples and yellows. But, interestingly, they cannot perceive red. Also, they never nectar in the shade; they need constant sunshine to keep their bodies warm. They simply cannot fly if the temperature drops below fifty-five degrees.

When it is flying weather, monarchs can cover up to eighty miles a day. They fly across the eastern United States, funnel through Texas, and then fan out across Mexico's Sierra Madre mountains. Then they begin to follow the mountain ranges that run north and south. They seek their winter refuges at altitudes of ten thousand feet in the transvolcanic mountains of central Mexico. Many years ago these mountains seethed with volcanic activity, but now their cones are flat and fir and pine forests have crept up their sides.

The Magic Circle

THIN RIVULETS of butterflies begin to stream into Mexico in early November. Their silhouettes are often spotted over cities and villages on the most festive of all days, the Days of the Dead, Las Días del Muertos. It is amidst life that the Mexicans celebrate and remember their departed friends and relatives. Graves are weeded, gravestones scrubbed and painted, and fresh flowers brought to decorate them. In homes, families make altars to welcome back the spirits of departed loved ones. And during these days in early November, it is believed by some that these spirits come on the wings of the monarch butterflies.

The returning monarchs need a special place to winter. It must be warm, but not so warm as to burn up all their fat supply. Nectaring flowers must be nearby, as well as a water source. There should be some exposure to sun, but also shelter from bitter cold and wind. These conditions create a smaller climate within a larger one—a microclimate.

Some people call this special place within a forest a "magic circle." There are less than a dozen magic circles so far known in all of Mexico.

In the canopy of the oyamel forests that grow on the sides of the mountains, monarchs congregate in immense colonies. But these colonies are threatened. Logging has long been an important industry for the poor villages at the base of the mountains. Some of the villages have no plumbing or electricity, and the land is not always good for growing food. The people depend on logging, and it is hard to tell them to stop the work that supports them. But if the oyamel forests are cut down, there will be nowhere for the monarchs to winter.

Bill Calvert is a scientist, and like many others he is worried about the future of the monarch. Bill has hundreds of questions about these butterflies. How do they fly? How do they navigate? How do they get where they are going? To try to answer these questions, he has tracked monarchs all across his home state of Texas right down into Mexico.

Several times a year, Bill travels to Mexico to study the monarchs and lead groups of interested people to the winter colonies. He hopes that tourism will replace logging as a source of income for the people of the mountain villages. At one of the largest monarch colonies of all, El Rosario, in the Mexican state of Michoacán, the people are trying to make the change.

El Rosario

"TORTILLAS, *quesadillas, sopa de pollo, tamales, enchiladas, tacos nopales, tacos con carne, papas y tacos.*" The woman sings out the menu from the back of the open-front shed where she stands at a small clay stove. An oil drum lid is set atop the clay stove, and thin flat tortillas made of blue corn flour sizzle in the hot oil.

Maria opened her lunch stand four years ago when the scientists and tourists started coming to El Rosario to see the *mariposas,* the butterflies, that roost in the trees just up the mountain. She also sells doilies, place mats, and small towels decorated with crocheted and embroidered designs of the monarchs. Across the rutted dirt road other villagers have built sheds from which butterfly T-shirts, jewelry, and postcards are sold. The people are trying to start new businesses and find new ways of earning money from tourism.

Almost everyone at El Rosario is trying to do something in this new business, and the government and conservation groups are helping them to start. Some people are guides, leading tourists up into the forests where the colony of millions upon millions of butterflies lives from November to March. Some people operate food stands; others sell souvenirs.

But El Rosario is not yet a tourist town. There is only one dirt street, and it is deeply rutted. At the top, it is barely wide enough for a truck before it peters out into a twisting pathway. When the mud-encrusted tourist buses come, they park at the bottom of the road. The people must walk up to the forest to see the butterflies. At this colony there is an admission fee, and visitors must stay on the paths. They cannot even pick up the dead butterflies.

The monarchs roost in the trees. They cover the branches and trunks so thickly that it is impossible to see the bark or the fir needles through them. On cool mornings their brightly colored wings are folded shut with the dull side out. They hang from the tree limbs in gigantic clusters like bunches of tissue-paper shingles.

If a night is too cold, butterflies on the outside of the clusters fall to the forest floor. This is dangerous. There is a bird in this forest that has figured out a way to avoid the milkweed poison that collects in the exoskeleton, or outer structure, of the butterfly. This bird simply "unzips" or splits open the monarch's body and scoops out the insides, leaving the poisonous skeleton behind. And the fallen butterflies not eaten by this bird may be gobbled by the mice that search the forest floor for food. Until the fallen monarchs are warm enough to fly, they remain in a state of suspended animation on the ground.

As the morning warms, the monarchs begin to move. An orange shiver spreads across the forest floor as they stir and begin to creep upward along any vertical surface, be it a tree root or a twig. Their instinct is to move up toward safety, away from the ground and into the protection of the forest canopy.

A small plant not more than a foot high is festooned with dozens of butterflies all clambering upward. They are still too cold for flying, but their legs are all working. Of the monarch's six legs, the first pair is the shortest and tucked up close to the butterfly's body. The other four are longer and are used for walking and latching on to things. These four legs have little backward-facing claws that help the monarchs grip tightly. And not only can these feet grip and clamber, but they can taste, too. The feet of a monarch are two thousand times more sensitive than human taste buds.

When the frigid little butterflies began their climb, they had no way of knowing that the stem of the plant would come to an end after ten inches.

If the monarchs had been on the trunk of an oyamel tree, they could have continued to climb sixty feet to safety. Instead they have dead-ended at the top of a very short plant. And it is still too cold to fly. They all stack up toward the ends of this twig, their wings jutting out at odd angles, like facets of a naturally growing crystal.

Unlike butterflies on the little plants, the monarchs that fell close to the trunk of a tree have a straight uninterrupted journey to safety in the canopy.

In the Rosario colony there are 3,489 trees, and it is estimated that this colony alone is the habitat for 30 to 40 million butterflies each winter.

La Herrada

ANOTHER MONARCH colony, smaller and not as well known as El Rosario, is near the village of Valle de Bravo. It is one of Bill's favorites. There are no guides, and a visitor can travel the twisting mountain paths alone. But the colony is hard to find. It is a smaller population of butterflies, only two or three million, on a large mountain, and it often relocates slightly from one year to the next.

Bill Calvert has not been here for a few years. He has trouble just finding the path up the mountain, and he has no idea where the colony might be. With him this time are five children and their parents, the same children who visited Clara Waterman on the island in Maine so many months before. They remember the butterfly they saw fly off Clara's porch. It seems unbelievable that the same butterfly could be here in Mexico, possibly on this very mountain.

The climb is not easy. The air is thin and the day is already warm. They stop often to drink from their canteens. By eleven o'clock, the children and their parents, with Bill in the lead, have walked up one thousand feet higher on the mountain. It has taken them almost two hours, but they have finally spotted their first butterflies, just a few flitting through the trees. Because the air is cooler this high on the mountain, every now and then a butterfly is found on the ground in a chilly stupor. Bill shows the children how to revive a cold monarch. He picks up the butterfly, very gently pinching both wings together. Then, cupping the butterfly in both hands, he blows softly on it. A few warm breaths are all that is needed. He opens his hands and a revived butterfly slips out, happy to be airborne again.

The children form rescue squads for downed butterflies and run ahead on the path giving first aid to the chilled monarchs.

But where is this main colony? Where are the roosting trees? It's hard to believe that three million butterflies can be so difficult to find.

The forest breaks open to a meadow, or *llano*, sprigged with wildflowers and bunch grass. There are monarchs flying about, nectaring on tiny colorful blossoms. But there is still no sign of the main colony. While the humans take a "nectar break" with sandwiches and sodas, Bill watches the sky. He is not looking

41

for more monarchs. Instead he is waiting for a cloud he has spotted in the distance moving toward the picnic site.

When a cloud passes over, monarchs panic. Their first instinct is to head back to the roost while they are still warm enough to fly. If they are feeding, they must get off the exposed ground because it loses heat very rapidly. If there is a drastic drop in temperature to below forty degrees, monarchs cannot even crawl.

As the shadow of the cloud slides over the meadow, the butterflies that had been darting and flitting about suddenly stream out of the meadow and into the forest. Bill and the children pack up as fast as they can and follow.

The fleeing monarchs head toward a magic circle deep in the mountain woods. Bill and the children race into the forest following the butterflies. They run past a bush with Japanese lantern flowers, past an air plant swinging high above the forest floor with its tiny yellow snow-flake blossoms. They scramble up a steep bank encrusted with moss. Fallen monarchs litter the ground.

"Look for the baskers!" Bill calls. "That will be the first sign. The show of orange wings in the trees with the first flash of sun as the cloud passes."

The way is choked with vines and brambles, but there are more and more butterflies — some on the soft forest floor, dead, chewed by mice; some still cold, not flying but stiffly walking on their jointed limbs; others flying in loops and gentle slants through the branches overhead, embroidering the air with their orange-and-black finery. The path gets steeper and more tangled. Gray hanging moss, wispy as old men's beards, blows in the breeze. Slender arcing stems spiked with thorns reach out to scratch the children's faces. And then the smallest child, who has run past Bill, gasps. Just ahead, millions of monarchs hang in immense clusters. The children stop and sit

directly under the trees. There are no rules here; they can sit as close as they want to the butterflies. But they are careful not to disturb them. They look up in wonder. It is a sudden autumn as the tree turns bright orange and half a million butterflies open their wings to greet a shaft of sunlight. For a brief instant the forest seems spun with gold as the sun continues to blast through and the monarchs bask, their wings open to catch its heat.

When the sun flash is over, the hanging monarchs close their wings once more, while others fly all around the children, landing on their heads, their knees, their shoulders.

Suddenly there is a cascade of monarchs right over their heads. In unison the butterflies let go of their perches and fall in an orange shower.

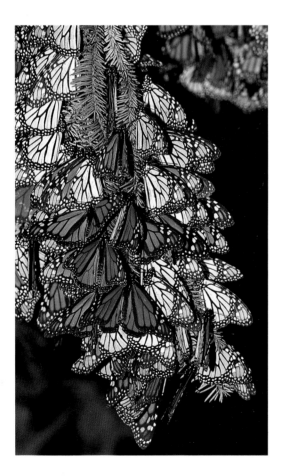

Bill explains that the monarchs have likely detected the carbon dioxide in the air from the children under them. When a human or any animal breathes, carbon dioxide is released. This triggers a startle reaction in the monarchs. It is thought by scientists that the first instinct of the monarchs after detecting the presence of carbon dioxide is to try to appear to be something other than an individual butterfly, something large and full of motion, not prey for a bird. As the butterflies cascade down onto the children's hair, faces, and shoulders, they seem like golden leaves blown by a gust of wind.

Bill Calvert tells the children an extraordinary story of a time there was a blizzard and more than a foot of snow covered the colony. Many of the monarchs died, but many also fell onto a snow-covered meadow. It snowed again, laying down a top blanket of snow. It was cold and sunless for several days, then one day the sun came out, quickly melting the top layer. From the white field there was a slow orange flutter upward as thousands of monarchs rose from the snow, unlocked at last from their frozen stupor.

In the late afternoon, as the first wisps of evening fog thread through the trees, the monarchs on the ground begin flying up. Within minutes it will be too chilly for them to fly, within hours too cold to even crawl. In clusters they will grow still in their brief spells of winter sleep, until the sun breaks through again.

Pacific Grove

"Y OU'VE GOT your hat on wrong."

"It's not my hat. It's my antennae!" The little girl scowls at the boy.

Ms. Klevan's kindergarten class is getting ready for one of the most exciting days of the school year: the second Saturday in October, the day of the butterfly parade. Pacific Grove is known as Butterfly Town, USA. It is one of several places on the coast of California where the monarchs come to winter. In early October when the butterflies west of the Rocky Mountains sweep in from the north, crossing the Sierra Nevada, Pacific Grove is ready. The parade is the town's way of welcoming the returning monarchs that will roost for the brief winter months in the two local groves of eucalyptus and pine. The children can hardly wait for parade day, and they run in practice flights waving their arms, their pipe-cleaner antennae jiggling.

On parade day morning, the children in Pacific Grove are up early and dressed in their costumes. Ms. Klevan is already at the parade's start with the big felt caterpillar banner the class will march behind. She makes sure that everyone's wings are secure and antennae in place. Everywhere

children are dressed as nectar flowers, striped caterpillars, and monarchs.

It's just minutes before the parade and antennae quiver in anticipation. At the first booming notes of the marching band the parade begins. Parents run alongside their caterpillar and butterfly children, taking pictures and cheering them on. People lining the streets burst

into applause. The streets undu-
late with a wave of bright orange-
and-black wings.

The marchers sing welcome
monarch songs as they pass
the reviewing stand where the
mayor, several butterfly scientists
from around the country, the
town council, and the president
of the Friends of the Monarch
society sit and wave at the hundreds of butterfly children.

Ro Vaccaro is president of the Friends of the Monarch. She has fought very hard to preserve the two monarch groves in town. One of these two habitats is privately owned, and the owner wanted to cut down many of the trees to build condominiums. The people of Pacific Grove were outraged. They knew it would be the end of their winter visitors who bring beauty and grace to their city every year. Along with other members of the Friends of the Monarch, Ro Vaccaro launched a campaign to save the grove. Through the city council they introduced a proposal for the town to buy the butterfly grove from the owner. In November when the voters went to the polls, they voted overwhelmingly to approve two million dollars for the purchase of the grove to save it from development.

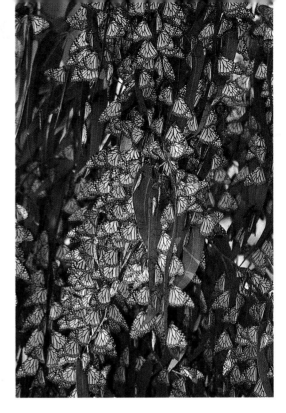

The owner then raised the price and Ro got mad. "The owner is holding the butterflies hostage!" she charged. The townspeople were angry, too. Finally the owner gave in and the town bought the grove.

The other grove is already owned by the town. It isn't threatened by developers, but by simple old age. Many of the eucalyptus trees have died. These trees are important in providing wind protection as well as shelters where the fog that rolls in from the Pacific Ocean can collect. If the butterflies do not get enough water, they dry out and die. Fog brings the moisture they need, and the warm water droplets of the foggy nights keep the air temperature from falling below freezing.

When trees die, holes are created in the magic circle, upsetting the fragile microclimate. The Friends of the Monarch again came to the rescue. They collected cones from Monterey pines. These cones were heated until they popped open, releasing eighty to ninety seeds. The seeds were then planted in small cups and are being raised in a greenhouse. When the new trees are about a foot tall, they will be planted in the grove to replace the ones that have died.

The people of Pacific Grove are very rich compared to the people at the base of the mountain in Mexico. They have time and they have money. They voted to raise their own taxes in order to buy the butterfly grove. And on their days off from work they plant seedlings in the town's other grove. They have time to argue with politicians and write letters. And they know the environment is as fragile as the tissue-paper–thin wings of the butterflies that bring beauty to their lives.

Before Ro Vaccaro moved to California she had lived in an eastern city and had visited Pacific Grove only once. Then one day when she was working high up in a glass skyscraper, a monarch fluttered by her twentieth-floor window on its way to Mexico. It stopped to rest on the ledge, and Ro stopped typing. She looked at it hard — its lovely black-veined wings, the sunlight streaming through the shimmering patchwork of orange. It seemed to radiate an irresistible joy. On that same day Ro quit her job, packed up her belongings, and moved to Pacific Grove, where she could live in the butterflies' presence for several months of each year.

To do this Ro gave up a lot. She took another job in Pacific Grove at a much lower salary, and she lives in a smaller apartment. Ro's life is very different now. Almost every day before and after work she goes to the butterfly groves. Her excitement begins when the scouts, the first arrivals, start coming in the early days of October. And she is sad toward the end of February when the mating season begins, knowing the butterflies will soon be leaving. She has even worked to get Butterfly Crossing signs on sidewalks and streets where the monarchs often tumble out of the sky as they mate. "Step on one butterfly," Ro says, "and you wipe out the next four generations!"

For nearly eight months the butterflies will vanish from Pacific Grove and El Rosario, two different towns that in many ways share very little—except one important thing: in both towns the people decided to make a place for beauty. Throughout the year the people have worked to protect the habitats for their winter visitors. They have slowed down logging in one town and saved a grove from development in another. In the late fall of each year, when the weather grows cold and the leaves turn, when growing things begin to die, the monarchs return in their streams of silent flight. Their appearance seems almost magical at this time, the dying time of year, their beauty rare. It is a beauty that has deeply touched the lives and spirits of the people of the two towns who have become the guardians of the monarchs' winter habitat, the protectors of these small pieces of earth.

The Flight North

Toward the end of February in Mexico and Pacific Grove the monarchs become more active. They are very thirsty by the end of the long winter months, and on particularly warm days they stream through the trees to find water. These monarchs, the migrants of the previous autumn, now at last begin to mate. They have waited longer than any of the three previous generations of monarchs before them. In spiraling upward flights the males pursue the females. They clasp in mid-air, often falling to the ground, where they complete their mating. The male then picks up the female and flies her to a nearby tree.

Both males and females might mate numerous times. After the mating cycle is over, the male dies. But the female, heavy with eggs, is driven by instinct northward to the nearest milkweed fields, where she begins to lay her eggs—after which she too will die. Thus the cycle starts once more. An egg, white and shiny, no bigger than the head of a pin, starts to grow on the leaf of a milkweed plant. In a few days there will be a caterpillar, in another few weeks a butterfly, which in turn will mate and fly northward laden with eggs, as did its mother of three or four weeks before. This first spring generation from Mexico will reach the southern gulf states in late April or May, depending on the weather conditions. The butterflies will have been laying eggs all along the way in meadows of milkweed. By June many second-generation butterflies will reach the mid-latitude states—Virginia, Missouri, Iowa, and Delaware. By early summer the third generation will reach the Great Lakes, the wide bays of New England, and the southern border of Canada. They will light in gardens to nectar and in fields to lay their eggs. And some will wait patiently in trees on lonely points that jut into the sea until the right wind comes along to take them to an island where for more than seventy years a woman has waited for them every summer.

They weigh less than a gram; they fly more than two thousand miles. The monarchs will live their brief lives and share their fragile beauty as long as there are flowers to nectar from, clear water to drink, and magic circles of trees in which to winter sleep.